This book belongs to

- -

Precut Primer

Precut quilts that make the grade!

by Barbara Groves & Mary Jacobson of Me and My Sister Designs

Me and My Sister Designs website and blog: www.meandmysisterdesigns.com

Precut quilts that make the grade

Designers: Barbara Groves & Mary Jacobson of Me and My Sister Designs

Quilting: Sharon Elsberry

Sewers: Lissa Alexander, Kathryn Clausen, Melissa Corry, Barbara Groves, Deborah Hawkins, Sarah Huechteman, Mary Jacobson, Kimberly Jolly and Sherri McConnell

Editor-in-Chief: Kimberly Jolly

Art Director: Sarah Price

Copy Editors: Cheryl Cohorn and Nova Birchfield

Photographers: Sarah Price and Jocelyn Ueng

A special thank you to Moda Fabrics for supplying the fabric and to Aurifil for supplying the thread used in this book.

Published by:
Fat Quarter Shop®, PO Box 1544, Manchaca, Texas 78652
www.FatQuarterShop.com
www.ItsSewEmma.com

ISBN: 978-0-9881749-6-2

Contents

Precuts 101

Charm Pack

Hi-De-Ho

Layer Cake

Fat Quarter Bundle

Fat Eighth Bundle

Jelly Roll

Mini Charm Pack

Mini Charm Pack:

Includes 42 - 2 ½" squares.

Great for postage stamp blocks and Irish chain blocks.

Charm Pack:

Includes 42 - 5" squares.

Great for four patch blocks and nine patch blocks.

Jelly Roll:

Includes 40 - 2 ½" x width of fabric strips.

Great for strip piecing, binding and rail fence blocks.

Layer Cake:

Includes 42 - 10" squares.

Great for half square triangles and square in a square blocks.

Fat Eighth Bundle:

Includes one 9" x 21" piece from the entire collection.
Great for anything!

Fat Quarter Bundle:

Includes one 18" x 21" piece from the entire collection.
Great for anything!

Tips from Barb & Mary

Before the bell rings, we have a handy little "cheat sheet" of tips for you. It's not really cheating, but it will help you get through your work a little easier!

1. Don't pre-wash your fabrics.

2. Begin each project with a new sewing machine needle.

3. Starch your fabrics before cutting. Starching while you piece tends to stretch the fabric out of shape.

4. When cutting a stack of more than two fabrics, press the stack with a warm iron to keep it from slipping. We never stack more than four fabrics at one time.

5. Either cut from the markings on your ruler or your mat; never switch back and forth. These markings can be different.

6. When threading your needle, wet the eye of the needle instead of the end of the thread. It's the easier way to do it.

7. Hold a piece of white paper behind your needle as you thread it. The paper makes it easier to see the eye of the needle.

8. Cut the end of the thread at an angle. This will also help it slip through the eye of the needle easier.

9. Before you start, make sure you are using an accurate quarter-inch seam. Test it by drawing a line ¼" away from the edge of an index card. Then adjust your seam accordingly.

10. When sewing with a precut, measure from the outer point of the pinked edge.

11. When it comes to pressing, there's no right or wrong. One of us prefers to press open, the other to one side, so just do what works for you.

12. Finger press your seams open before pressing with an iron. This may save your fingers.

13. Use a piece of tape wrapped around your finger, sticky side out, to remove stray threads after ripping out a seam.

14. Make your binding right after you finish your quilt top. Then store it until your quilt is ready to be bound.

15. Roll a lint roller over the surface of your cutting mat for a quick clean-up.

Now that you are prepped and ready, let's head to class!

Barb in 7th grade.

Barb in 12th grade.

Mary in 3rd grade.

Mary in 10th grade.

1st Grade Quilt

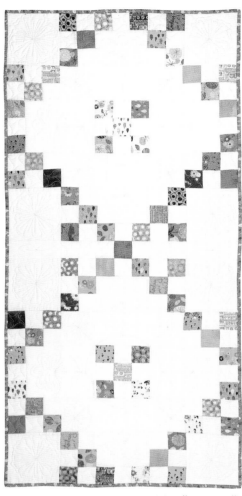

26 ½" x 54 ½"

Fabric Requirements:

Fabrics	Quantity	Description
A	75 - 2 ½" squares	Two Moda Mini Charm Packs
B to G	1 ½ yards	Background
H	½ yard	Binding
	1 ¾ yards	Backing

Cutting Instructions:

Mini Charm Packs	75 - 2 ½" squares (A)
Background	3 - 6 ½" x 42" strips, subcut into:
	4 - 6 ½" x 8 ½" rectangles (B)
	8 - 6 ½" squares (C)
	3 - 4 ½" x 42" strips, subcut into:
	4 - 4 ½" x 14 ½" rectangles (D)
	4 - 4 ½" x 6 ½" rectangles (E)
	5 - 2 ½" x 42" strips, subcut into:
	2 - 2 ½" x 12 ½" rectangles (F)
	64 - 2 ½" squares (G)
Binding	5 - 2 ¼" x 42" strips (H)

The 1st Grade Quilt features the Mon Ami collection by BasicGrey for Moda Fabrics.

Piecing Instructions:

1st Grade Blocks:

Assemble five Fabric A squares and four Fabric G squares.

1st Grade Nine Patch Block should measure 6 ½" x 6 ½".

Make two.

Make two.

Assemble three Fabric A squares and three Fabric G squares.

1st Grade Six Patch Block should measure 4 ½" x 6 ½".

Make sixteen.

Make sixteen.

Assemble two Fabric A squares and one Fabric G square.

1st Grade Three Patch Unit should measure 2 ½" x 6 ½".

Make eight.

Make eight.

Assemble one 1st Grade Three Patch Unit and one Fabric E rectangle.

1st Grade Three Patch Block should measure ½" x 6 ½".

Make four.

Make four.

Quilt Center:

Assemble the Quilt Center.

Pay close attention to block placement.

Quilt Center should measure 26 ½" x 54 ½".

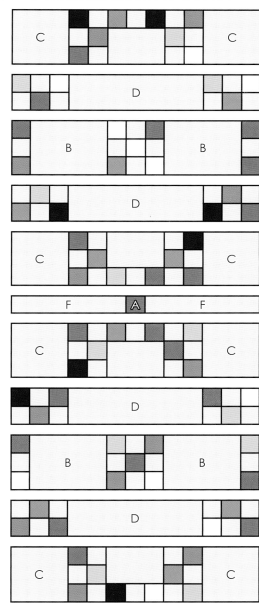

Finishing:

Piece the Fabric H strips end to end for binding.

Quilt and bind as desired.

2nd Grade Quilt

21 ½" x 26 ½"

Fabric Requirements:

Fabrics	Quantity	Description
A	80 - 2 ½" squares	Two Moda Mini Charm Packs
B to F	1 yard	Background
G	⅜ yard	Binding
	⅞ yard	Backing

Cutting Instructions:

Mini Charm Packs	80 - 2 ½" squares (A)
Background	3 - 4 ½" x 42" strips, subcut into:
	20 - 4 ½" squares (B)
	9 - 1 ½" x 42" strips, subcut into:
	16 - 1 ½" x 4 ½" rectangles (C)
	3 - 1 ½" x 24 ½" strips (D)
	2 - 1 ½" x 24 ½" strips (E)
	2 - 1 ½" x 21 ½" strips (F)
Binding	4 - 2 ¼" x 42" strips (G)

The 2nd Grade Quilt features the Hi-De-Ho collection by Me and My Sister Designs for Moda Fabrics.

Piecing Instructions:

2nd Grade Blocks:

Draw a diagonal line on the wrong side of the Fabric A squares.

With right sides facing, layer a Fabric A square on one corner of a Fabric B square.

Stitch on the drawn line and trim ¼" away from the seam.

Make twenty.

Repeat on the remaining corners of the Fabric B square.

2nd Grade Block should measure 4 ½" x 4 ½".

Make twenty.

Make twenty.

Quilt Center:

Assemble the Quilt Center.

Quilt Center should measure 19 ½" x 24 ½".

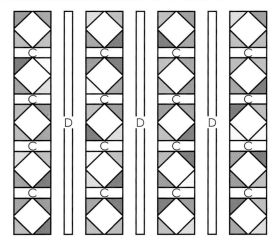

Borders:

Attach side borders using the Fabric E strips.

Attach top and bottom borders using the Fabric F strips.

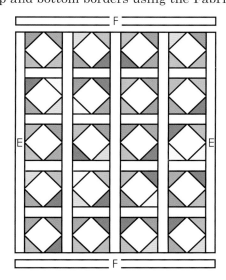

Finishing:

Piece the Fabric G strips end to end for binding.

Quilt and bind as desired.

3rd Grade Quilt

29" x 33 ¾"

Fabric Requirements:

Fabrics	Quantity	Description
A & B	42 - 5" squares	One Moda Charm Pack
C to E	1 ¼ yards	Background
F	⅜ yard	Binding
	1 yard	Backing

Cutting Instructions:

Charm Pack — Cut each charm pack square into:

2 - 2 ⅜" squares (A)

4 - 1 ¼" x 2 ¼" rectangles (B)

Background — 6 - 2 ⅜" x 42" strips, subcut into:

84 - 2 ⅜" squares (C)

9 - 2 ¼" x 42" strips, subcut into:

42 - 2 ¼" squares (D)

168 - 1 ¼" x 2 ¼" rectangles (E)

Binding — 4 - 2 ¼" x 42" strips (F)

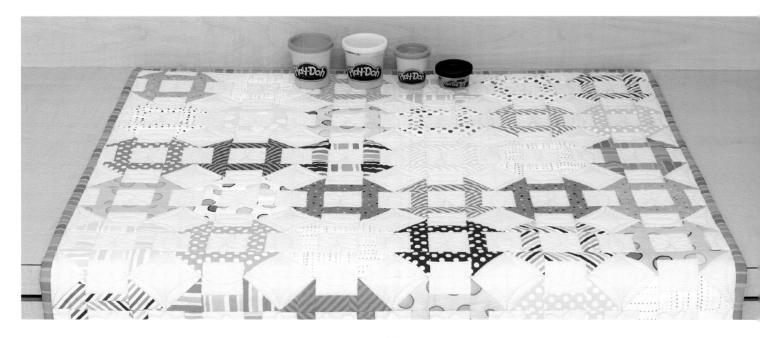

The 3rd Grade Quilt features the Dot Dot Dash collection by Me and My Sister Designs for Moda Fabrics.

Piecing Instructions:

3rd Grade Blocks:

Draw a diagonal line on the wrong side of the Fabric C squares.

With right sides facing, layer a Fabric C square with a Fabric A square.

Stitch ¼" from each side of the drawn line.

Cut apart on the marked line.

Half Square Triangle Unit should measure 2" x 2".

Make one hundred sixty-eight.

Make one hundred sixty-eight.

Assemble one Fabric E rectangle and one Fabric B rectangle.

Rectangle Unit should measure 2" x 2 ¼".

Make one hundred sixty-eight.

Make one hundred sixty-eight.

Assemble four matching Half Square Triangle Units, four matching Rectangle Units and one Fabric D square.

3rd Grade Block should measure 5 ¼" x 5 ¼".

Make forty-two.

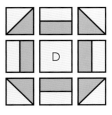 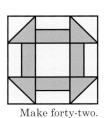

Make forty-two.

Quilt Center:

Assemble the Quilt Center.

Quilt Center should measure 29" x 33 ¾".

Finishing:

Piece the Fabric F strips end to end for binding.

Quilt and bind as desired.

4th Grade Quilt

24 ½" x 28 ½"

Fabric Requirements:

Fabrics	Quantity	Description
A & B	42 - 5" squares	One Moda Charm Pack
C to E	1 ¼ yards	Background
F	⅜ yard	Binding
	⅞ yard	Backing

Cutting Instructions:

Charm Pack	Cut each charm pack square into:
	1 - 2 ½" x 4 ½" rectangle (A)
	2 - 1 ½" x 2 ½" rectangles (B)

Background

10 - 2 ½" x 42" strips, subcut into:

    84 - 2 ½" squares (C)

    84 - 1 ½" x 2 ½" rectangles (D)

7 - 1 ½" x 42" strips, subcut into:

    168 - 1 ½" squares (E)

Binding 4 - 2 ¼" x 42" strips (F)

The 4th Grade Quilt features the Gooseberry collection by Lella Boutique for Moda Fabrics.

Piecing Instructions:

4th Grade Blocks:

Draw a diagonal line on the wrong side of the Fabric E squares.

With right sides facing, layer a Fabric E square on the top end of a Fabric B rectangle.

Stitch on the drawn line and trim ¼" away from the seam.

Make eighty-four.

Repeat on the bottom end of the Fabric B rectangle.

Small Flying Geese Unit should measure 1 ½" x 2 ½".

Make eighty-four.

Make eighty-four.

Draw a diagonal line on the wrong side of the Fabric C squares.

With right sides facing, layer a Fabric C square on the top end of a Fabric A rectangle.

Stitch on the drawn line and trim ¼" away from the seam.

Make forty-two.

Repeat on the bottom end of the Fabric A rectangle.

Large Flying Geese Unit should measure 2 ½" x 4 ½".

Make forty-two.

Make forty-two.

Assemble the 4th Grade Block.

4th Grade Block should measure 4 ½" x 4 ½".

Make forty-two.

Make forty-two.

Quilt Center:

Assemble the Quilt Center.

Quilt Center should measure 24 ½" x 28 ½".

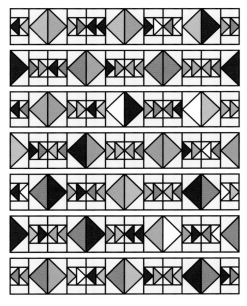

Finishing:

Piece the Fabric F strips end to end for binding.

Quilt and bind as desired.

5th Grade Quilt

74 ¾" x 89 ½"

Fabric Requirements:

Fabrics	Quantity	Description
A to F	36 - 2 ½" x 42" strips	One Moda Jelly Roll
G to N	4 ⅞ yards	Background
O	⅞ yard	Binding
	5 ½ yards	Backing

Cutting Instructions:

Jelly Roll Cut each jelly roll strip into:

1 - 2 ½" x 3" rectangle (A)

1 - 2 ½" x 5" rectangle (B)

1 - 2 ½" x 6" rectangle (C)

1 - 2 ½" x 8" rectangle (D)

1 - 2 ½" x 9" rectangle (E)

1 - 2 ½" x 11" rectangle (F)

2 ½" [A B C D E F] 42"

Background 3 - 3" x 42" strips, subcut into:

36 - 3" squares (G)

28 - 1 ½" x 42" strips, subcut into:

36 - 1 ½" x 5" rectangles (H)

36 - 1 ½" x 6" rectangles (I)

36 - 1 ½" x 8" rectangles (J)

36 - 1 ½" x 9" rectangles (K)

3 - 16 ⅛" x 42" strips, subcut into:

5 - 16 ⅛" squares (L)

5 - 11" x 42" strips, subcut into:

14 - 11" squares (M)

1 - 8 ⅜" x 42" strip, subcut into:

2 - 8 ⅜" squares (N)

Binding 10 - 2 ¼" x 42" strips (O)

The 5th Grade Quilt features the Dot Dot Dash collection by Me and My Sister Designs for Moda Fabrics.

Piecing Instructions:

5th Grade Blocks:

Assemble one Fabric A rectangle, one Fabric G square and one matching Fabric B rectangle.

5th Grade Unit A should measure 5" x 5".

Make thirty-six.

Make thirty-six.

Assemble one Fabric H rectangle, one 5th Grade Unit A and one Fabric I rectangle.

5th Grade Unit B should measure 6" x 6".

Make thirty-six.

Make thirty-six.

Assemble one Fabric C rectangle, one matching 5th Grade Unit B and one matching Fabric D rectangle.

5th Grade Unit C should measure 8" x 8".

Make thirty-six.

Make thirty-six.

Assemble one Fabric J rectangle, one 5th Grade Unit C and one Fabric K rectangle.

5th Grade Unit D should measure 9" x 9".

Make thirty-six.

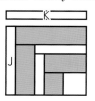 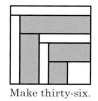

Make thirty-six.

Assemble one Fabric E rectangle, one matching 5th Grade Unit D and one matching Fabric F rectangle.

5th Grade Block should measure 11" x 11".

Make thirty-six.

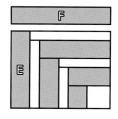 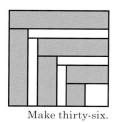

Make thirty-six.

Corner and Setting Triangles:

Cut the Fabric N squares on the diagonal once.

Make four.

Make four.

Cut the Fabric L squares on the diagonal twice.

Make twenty.

You will not use two Fabric L triangles.

Make twenty.

Quilt Center:

Assemble the Quilt Center.

Trim Quilt Center to measure 74 ¾" x 89 ½".

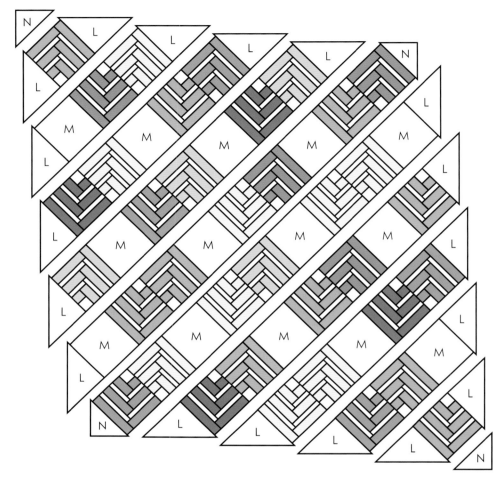

Finishing:

Piece the Fabric O strips end to end for binding.

Quilt and bind as desired.

6th Grade Quilt

78 ½" x 78 ½"

Fabric Requirements:

Fabrics	Quantity	Description
A to F	36 - 2 ½" x 42" strips	One Moda Jelly Roll
G to L	5 yards	Background
M	¾ yard	Binding
	7 ⅜ yards	Backing

Cutting Instructions:

Jelly Roll	Cut each jelly roll strip into:
	1 - 2 ½" x 6" rectangle (A)
	1 - 2 ½" x 8" rectangle (B)
	1 - 2 ½" x 6" rectangle (C)
	1 - 2 ½" x 8" rectangle (D)
	1 - 2 ½" x 6" rectangle (E)
	1 - 2 ½" x 8" rectangle (F)

2 ½" [A | B | C | D | E | F]
42"

Background	6 - 5 ¾" x 42" strips, subcut into:
	36 - 5 ¾" squares (G)
	29 - 1 ½" x 42" strips, subcut into:
	36 - 1 ½" x 7" rectangles (H)
	36 - 1 ½" x 7" rectangles (I)
	36 - 1 ½" x 7" rectangles (J)
	36 - 1 ½" x 7" rectangles (K)
	9 - 10" x 42" strips, subcut into:
	36 - 10" squares (L)
Binding	9 - 2 ¼" x 42" strips (M)

The 6th Grade Quilt features the Hi-De-Ho collection by Me and My Sister Designs for Moda Fabrics.

Piecing Instructions:

6th Grade Blocks:

Assemble one Fabric A rectangle, one Fabric G square and one matching Fabric B rectangle.

6th Grade Unit A should measure an undersized 8" x 8".

Make thirty-six.

 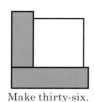

Make thirty-six.

Assemble one Fabric H rectangle, one 6th Grade Unit A and one Fabric I rectangle.

6th Grade Unit B should measure an undersized 9" x 9".

Make thirty-six.

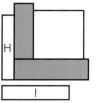 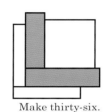

Make thirty-six.

Assemble one Fabric C rectangle, one matching 6th Grade Unit B and one matching Fabric D rectangle.

6th Grade Unit C should measure an undersized 11" x 11".

Make thirty-six.

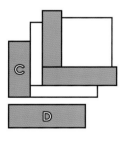 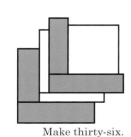

Make thirty-six.

Assemble one Fabric J rectangle, one 6th Grade Unit C and one Fabric K rectangle.

6th Grade Unit D should measure an undersized 12" x 12".

Make thirty-six.

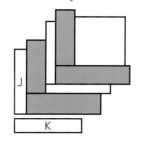 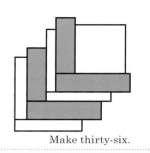

Make thirty-six.

Assemble one Fabric E rectangle, one matching 6th Grade Unit D and one matching Fabric F rectangle.

6th Grade Unit E should measure an undersized 14" x 14".

Make thirty-six.

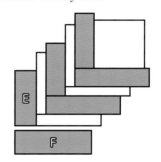 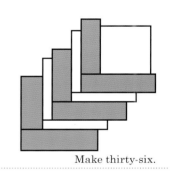

Make thirty-six.

Using the 45 degree diagonal line on your ruler, trim 3 ½" away from the center of each 6th Grade Unit E.

Partial 6th Grade Unit should measure approximately 7" x 18 ⅞".

Make thirty-six.

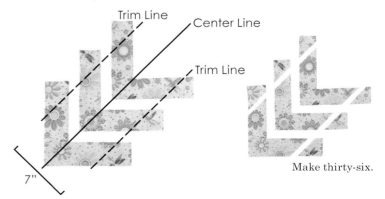

Make thirty-six.

Cut the Fabric L squares on the diagonal once.

Make seventy-two.

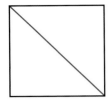 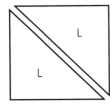

Make seventy-two.

Assemble two Fabric L triangles to one Partial 6th Grade Unit by matching centers for placement.

Make thirty-six Unfinished 6th Grade Units.

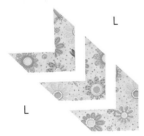

Make thirty-six.

Using the print fabric on the bottom as a guide, trim the 6th Grade Block to measure 13 ½" x 13 ½".

Make thirty-six.

Make thirty-six.

Quilt Rows:

Assemble six 6th Grade Blocks.

Quilt Row should measure 13 ½" x 78 ½".

Make six.

Make six.

Quilt Center:

Assemble the Quilt Center.

Quilt Center should measure 78 ½" x 78 ½".

Finishing:

Piece the Fabric M strips end to end for binding.

Quilt and bind as desired.

7th Grade Quilt

60 ½" x 70 ½"

Fabric Requirements:

Fabrics	Quantity	Description
A & B	42 - 10" squares	One Moda Layer Cake
C to E	3 ⅞ yards	Background
F	¾ yard	Binding
	4 yards	Backing

Cutting Instructions:

Layer Cake	Cut each layer cake square into:
	2 - 4 ⅞" squares (A)
	4 - 2 ½" x 4 ½" rectangles (B)

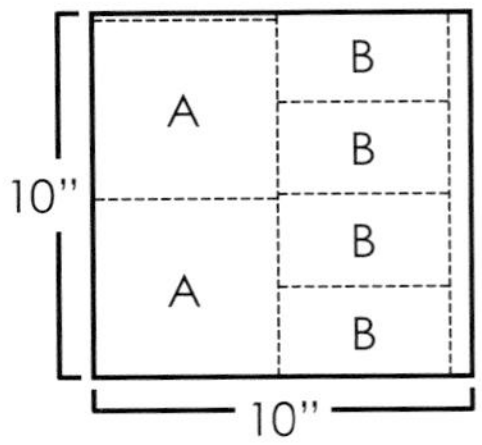

Background	11 - 4 ⅞" x 42" strips, subcut into:
	84 - 4 ⅞" squares (C)
	3 - 2 ½" x 42" strips, subcut into:
	42 - 2 ½" squares (D)
	34 - 2" x 42" strips, subcut into:
	672 - 2" squares (E)
Binding	8 - 2 ¼" x 42" strips (F)

The 7th Grade Quilt features the Hi-De-Ho collection by Me and My Sister Designs for Moda Fabrics.

Piecing Instructions:

7th Grade Blocks:

Draw a diagonal line on the wrong side of the Fabric C squares.

With right sides facing, layer a Fabric C square with a Fabric A square.

Stitch ¼" from each side of the drawn line.

Cut apart on the marked line.

Half Square Triangle Unit should measure 4 ½" x 4 ½".

Make one hundred sixty-eight.

Make one hundred sixty-eight.

Draw a diagonal line on the wrong side of the Fabric E squares.

With right sides facing, layer a Fabric E square on the top left corner and the bottom right corner of a Fabric B rectangle.

Stitch on the drawn lines and trim ¼" away from the seam.

Make one hundred sixty-eight.

Repeat on the remaining corners of the Fabric B rectangle.

Rectangle Unit should measure 2 ½" x 4 ½".

Make one hundred sixty-eight.

Make one hundred sixty-eight.

Assemble four matching Half Square Triangle Units, four matching Rectangle Units and one Fabric D square.

7th Grade Block should measure 10 ½" x 10 ½".

Make forty-two.

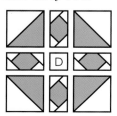   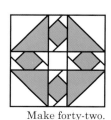

Make forty-two.

Quilt Center:

Assemble the Quilt Center.

Quilt Center should measure 60 ½" x 70 ½".

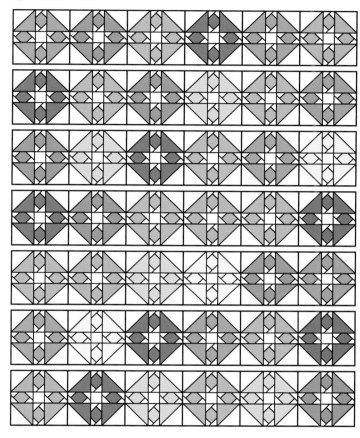

Finishing:

Piece the Fabric F strips end to end for binding.

Quilt and bind as desired.

8th Grade Quilt

64" x 75 ½"

Fabric Requirements:

Fabrics	Quantity	Description
A to C	30 - 10" squares	One Moda Layer Cake
D to J	3 ⅝ yards	Background, Sashing and Inner Border
K & L	1 ¼ yards	Outer Border
M	¾ yard	Binding
	4 ¾ yards	Backing

Cutting Instructions:

Layer Cake   Cut each layer cake square into:

> 4 - 3 ¼" squares (A)
>
> 4 - 2 ½" squares (B)
>
> 1 - 2" square (C)

Background   10 - 3 ¼" x 42" strips, subcut into:

> 120 - 3 ¼" squares (D)

8 - 2 ½" x 42" strips, subcut into:

> 120 - 2 ½" squares (E)

15 - 2" x 42" strips, subcut into:

> 120 - 2" x 4 ½" rectangles (F)

Sashing   8 - 1 ½" x 42" strips, subcut into:

> 30 - 1 ½" x 10" rectangles (G)

7 - 1 ½" x 42" strips, sew strips end to end and subcut into:

> 4 - 1 ½" x 63 ½" strips (H)

Inner Border   7 - 2 ½" x 42" strips, sew strips end to end and subcut into:

> 2 - 2 ½" x 63 ½" strips (I)
>
> 2 - 2 ½" x 56" strips (J)

Outer Border   8 - 4 ½" x 42" strips, sew strips end to end and subcut into:

> 2 - 4 ½" x 67 ½" strips (K)
>
> 2 - 4 ½" x 64" strips (L)

Binding   8 - 2 ¼" x 42" strips (M)

24

The 8th Grade Quilt features the Prairie collection by Corey Yoder for Moda Fabrics.

Piecing Instructions:

8th Grade Blocks:

For each 8th Grade Block, pair two coordinating layer cake fabrics.

Draw a diagonal line on the wrong side of the Fabric D squares.

With right sides facing, layer a Fabric D square with a Fabric A square.

Stitch ¼" from each side of the drawn line.

Cut apart on the marked line.

Half Square Triangle Unit should measure 2 ⅞" x 2 ⅞".

Make two hundred forty.

Make two hundred forty.

With right sides facing, layer two matching Half Square Triangle Units.

Make sure they are turned so that the seams are in the same direction.

Make one hundred twenty Paired Half Square Triangle Units.

Make one hundred twenty.

Draw diagonal lines ¼" away from the center on the wrong side of one of the Half Square Triangle Units in the opposite direction of the sewn seams. Using a ½" x 6" ruler is helpful.

Stitch on the two drawn lines and cut apart between the stitched lines.

Quarter Square Triangle Unit should measure 2 ½" x 2 ½".

Make two hundred forty.

Make two hundred forty.

Assemble one Fabric E square, two matching Quarter Square Triangle Units and one coordinating Fabric B square.

Pay close attention to unit placement.

8th Grade Unit should measure 4 ½" x 4 ½".

Make one hundred twenty.

Make one hundred twenty.

Assemble four matching 8th Grade Units, four Fabric F rectangles and one matching Fabric C square.

8th Grade Block should measure 10" x 10".

Make thirty.

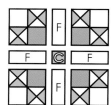 

Make thirty.

Quilt Center:

Assemble the Quilt Center.

Quilt Center should measure 52" x 63 ½".

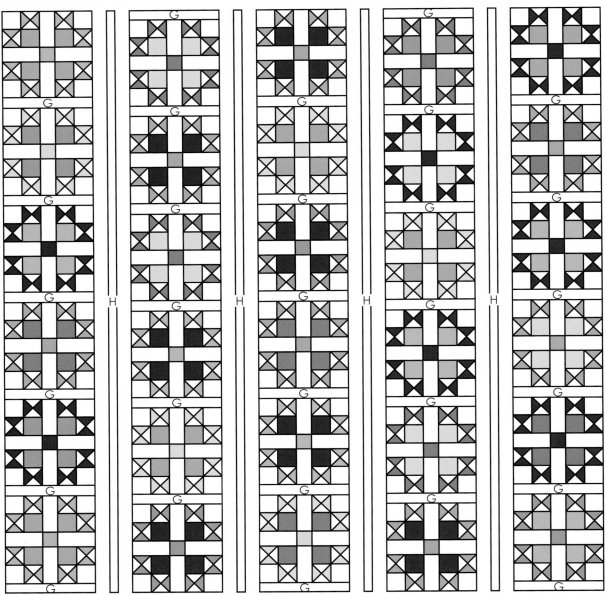

Borders:

Attach side inner borders using the Fabric I strips. Attach top and bottom inner borders using the Fabric J strips.
Attach side outer borders using the Fabric K strips. Attach top and bottom outer borders using the Fabric L strips.

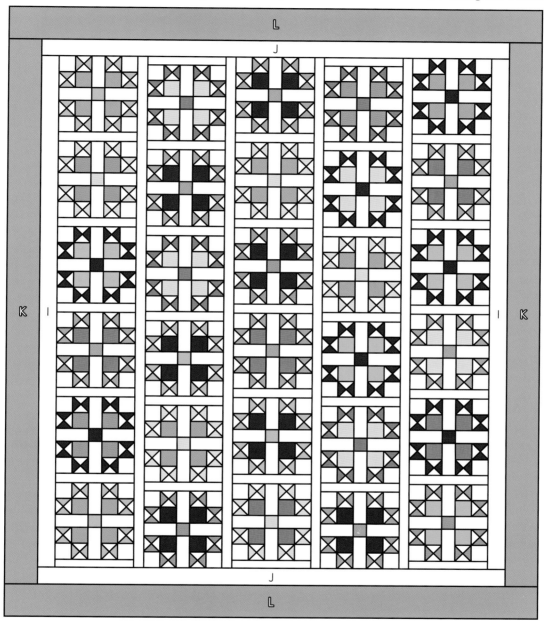

Finishing:

Piece the Fabric M strips end to end for binding.

Quilt and bind as desired.

9th Grade Quilt

60 ½" x 72 ½"

Fabric Requirements:

Fabrics	Quantity	Description
A & B	30 - 9" x 21" rectangles	30 Fat Eighths
C & D	2 ¾ yards	Background
E	¾ yard	Binding
	4 yards	Backing

Cutting Instructions:

Fat Eighths	Cut each fat eighth into:

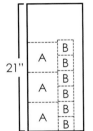

3 - 4 ⅞" squares (A)

6 - 2 ½" squares (B)

Background 12 - 4 ⅞" x 42" strips, subcut into:

90 - 4 ⅞" squares (C)

12 - 2 ½" x 42" strips, subcut into:

180 - 2 ½" squares (D)

Binding 8 - 2 ¼" x 42" strips (E)

The 9th Grade Quilt features the Farmhouse collection by Fig Tree Quilts for Moda Fabrics.

Piecing Instructions:

9th Grade Blocks:

Assemble two matching Fabric B squares and two Fabric D squares.

Four Patch Unit should measure 4 ½" x 4 ½".

Make ninety.

Make ninety.

Draw a diagonal line on the wrong side of the Fabric C squares.

With right sides facing, layer a Fabric C square with a Fabric A square.

Stitch ¼" from each side of the drawn line.

Cut apart on the marked line.

Half Square Triangle Unit should measure 4 ½" x 4 ½".

Make one hundred eighty.

Make one hundred eighty.

Assemble three matching Four Patch Units and six matching Half Square Triangle Units.

Pay close attention to unit placement.

9th Grade Block should measure 12 ½" x 12 ½".

Make thirty.

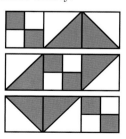 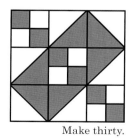

Make thirty.

Quilt Center:

Assemble the Quilt Center.

Pay close attention to block placement.

Quilt Center should measure 60 ½" x 72 ½".

Finishing:

Piece the Fabric E strips end to end for binding.

Quilt and bind as desired.

10th Grade Quilt

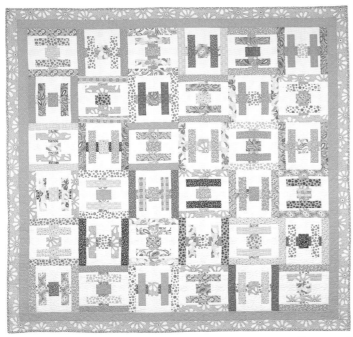

68 ½" x 68 ½"

Fabric Requirements:

Fabrics	Quantity	Description
A to D	36 - 9" x 21" rectangles	36 Fat Eighths
E to G	2 ½ yards	Background
H & I	⅝ yard	Inner Border
J & K	¾ yard	Outer Border
L	¾ yard	Binding
	4 ⅜ yards	Backing

Cutting Instructions:

Fat Eighths   Cut each fat eighth into:

    2 - 2" x 10 ½" rectangles (A)

    2 - 2" x 7 ½" rectangles (B)

    1 - 2 ½" x 4 ½" rectangle (C)

    1 - 2 ½" x 3 ½" rectangle (D)

Background   9 - 4 ½" x 42" strips, subcut into:

    72 - 4 ½" squares (E)

    8 - 2 ½" x 42" strips, subcut into:

    72 - 2 ½" x 4" rectangles (F)

    8 - 2" x 42" strips, subcut into:

    144 - 2" squares (G)

Inner Border   7 - 2 ½" x 42" strips, sew strips end to end and subcut into:

    2 - 2 ½" x 60 ½" strips (H)

    2 - 2 ½" x 64 ½" strips (I)

Outer Border   8 - 2 ½" x 42" strips, sew strips end to end and subcut into:

    2 - 2 ½" x 64 ½" strips (J)

    2 - 2 ½" x 68 ½" strips (K)

Binding   8 - 2 ¼" x 42" strips (L)

The 10th Grade Quilt features the Bandana collection by Me and My Sister Designs for Moda Fabrics.

Piecing Instructions:

10th Grade Blocks:

For each 10th Grade Block, pair four coordinating fat eighths.

Assemble two Fabric E squares and one Fabric C rectangle.

10th Grade Strip Set should measure 4 ½" x 10 ½".

Make thirty-six.

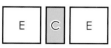 

Make thirty-six.

Subcut each 10th Grade Strip Set into four 1" x 10 ½" rectangles.

10th Grade Unit One should measure 1" x 10 ½".

Make one hundred forty-four.

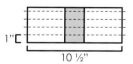 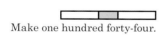

Make one hundred forty-four.

Assemble two Fabric G squares and one Fabric B rectangle.

10th Grade Unit Two should measure 2" x 10 ½".

Make seventy-two.

Make seventy-two.

Assemble two Fabric F rectangles and one Fabric D rectangle.

10th Grade Unit Three should measure 2 ½" x 10 ½".

Make thirty-six.

 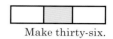

Make thirty-six.

Assemble two matching Fabric A rectangles, four coordinating matching 10th Grade Unit Ones, two coordinating matching 10th Grade Unit Twos and one coordinating 10th Grade Unit Three.

10th Grade Block should measure 10 ½" x 10 ½".

Make thirty-six.

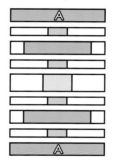 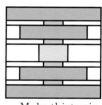

Make thirty-six.

Quilt Center:

Assemble the Quilt Center.

Quilt Center should measure 60 ½" x 60 ½".

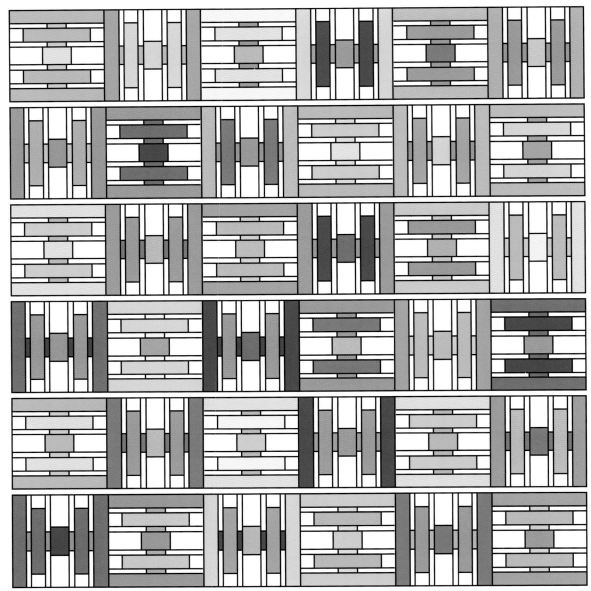

Borders:

Attach side inner borders using the Fabric H strips. Attach top and bottom inner borders using the Fabric I strips. Attach side outer borders using the Fabric J strips. Attach top and bottom outer borders using the Fabric K strips.

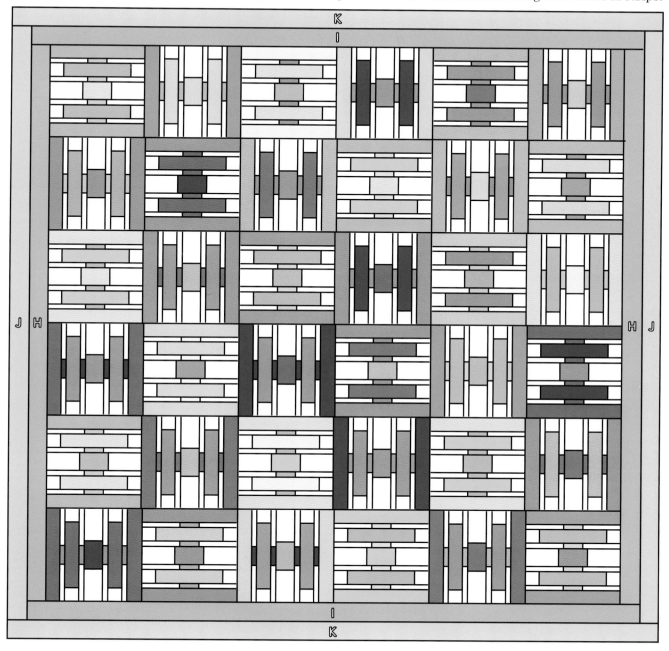

Finishing:

Piece the Fabric L strips end to end for binding.

Quilt and bind as desired.

11th Grade Quilt

80 ½" x 101"

Fabric Requirements:

Fabrics	Quantity	Description
A to E	32 - 18" x 21" rectangles	32 Fat Quarters
F to O	5 ½ yards	Background
P	⅞ yard	Binding
	7 ⅝ yards	Backing

Cutting Instructions:

Fat Quarters   Cut each fat quarter into:

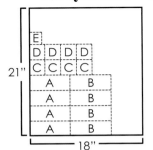

    4 - 2 ½" x 6 ½" rectangles (A)

    4 - 2 ½" x 6 ½" rectangles (B)

    4 - 2 ½" squares (C)

    4 - 2 ½" squares (D)

    1 - 1 ½" square (E)

Background   24 - 2 ½" x 42" strips, subcut into:

    256 - 2 ½" squares (F)

    128 - 2 ½" squares (G)

8 - 2" x 42" strips, subcut into:

    24 - 2" x 13 ½" rectangles (H)

22 - 1 ½" x 42" strips, subcut into:

    128 - 1 ½" x 6 ½" rectangles (I)

15 - 2" x 42" strips, sew strips end to end and subcut into:

    1 - 2" x 116 ½" strip (J)

    2 - 2" x 100 ½" strips (K)

    2 - 2" x 71 ½" strips (L)

    2 - 2" x 42 ½" strips (M)

2 - 19 ¾" x 42" strips, subcut into:

    4 - 19 ¾" squares (N)

1 - 10 ⅛" x 42" strip, subcut into:

    2 - 10 ⅛" squares (O)

Binding   11 - 2 ¼" x 42" strips (P)

The 11th Grade Quilt features the Hello Darling collection by Bonnie & Camille for Moda Fabrics.

Piecing Instructions:

11th Grade Blocks:

For each 11th Grade Block, pair two coordinating fat quarters.

Draw a diagonal line on the wrong side of the Fabric F squares.

With right sides facing, layer a Fabric F square on the bottom end of a Fabric A rectangle.

Stitch on the drawn line and trim ¼" away from the seam.

Left 11th Grade Unit should measure 2 ½" x 6 ½".

Make one hundred twenty-eight.

Make one hundred twenty-eight.

Assemble one Fabric C square, one Fabric G square and one coordinating Fabric D square.

Center 11th Grade Unit should measure 2 ½" x 6 ½".

Make one hundred twenty-eight.

Make one hundred twenty-eight.

With right sides facing, layer a Fabric F square on the top end of a Fabric B rectangle.

Stitch on the drawn line and trim ¼" away from the seam.

Right 11th Grade Unit should measure 2 ½" x 6 ½".

Make one hundred twenty-eight.

Make one hundred twenty-eight.

Assemble one Left 11th Grade Unit, one coordinating Center 11th Grade Unit and one coordinating Right 11th Grade Unit.

11th Grade Unit should measure 6 ½" x 6 ½".

Make one hundred twenty-eight.

Make one hundred twenty-eight.

Assemble four matching 11th Grade Units, four Fabric I rectangles and one coordinating Fabric E square.

11th Grade Block should measure 13 ½" x 13 ½".

Make thirty-two.

 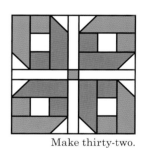
Make thirty-two.

Quilt Rows:

Cut the Fabric N squares on the diagonal twice.

Make sixteen.

You will not use two Fabric N triangles.

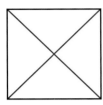 

Make sixteen.

Cut the Fabric O squares on the diagonal once.

Make four.

Make four.

Assemble two Fabric N triangles and one 11th Grade Block.

Make two.

   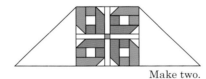

Make two.

Assemble two Fabric N triangles, three 11th Grade Blocks and two Fabric H rectangles.

Make two.

     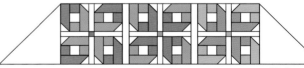

Make two

Assemble two Fabric N triangles, five 11th Grade Blocks and four Fabric H rectangles.

Make two.

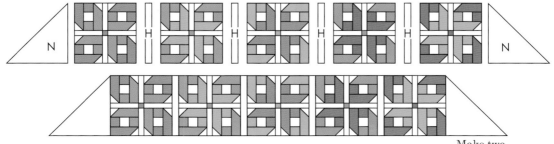

Make two.

Assemble one Fabric N triangle, seven 11th Grade Blocks, six Fabric H rectangles and one Fabric O triangle. Make two.

Make two.

Quilt Center:
Assemble the Quilt Center.
Trim Quilt Center to measure 80 ½" x 101".

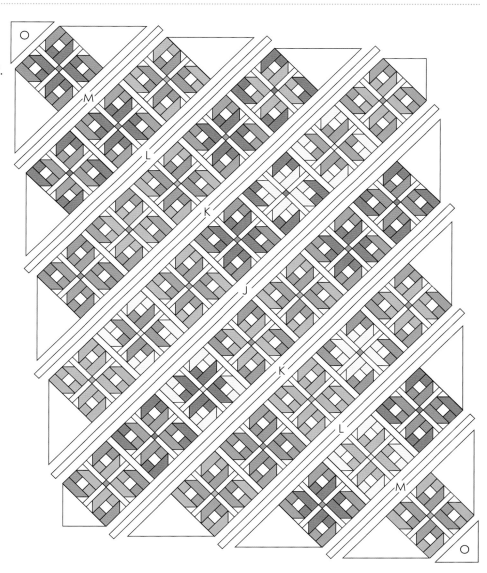

Finishing:
Piece the Fabric P strips end to end for binding.
Quilt and bind as desired.

12th Grade Quilt

87 ½" x 94 ½"

Fabric Requirements:

Fabrics	Quantity	Description
A to D	30 - 18" x 21" rectangles	30 Fat Quarters
E & F	1 ¼ yards	Accent
G to L	4 ⅛ yards	Background
M	⅞ yard	Binding
	8 ⅛ yards	Backing

Cutting Instructions:

Fat Quarters Cut each fat quarter into:

4 - 4 ¼" squares (A)

4 - 4 ¼" squares (B)

4 - 3" squares (C)

8 - 1 ¾" squares (D)

Accent 11 - 3" x 42" strips, subcut into:

30 - 3" x 8" rectangles (E)

60 - 3" squares (F)

Background 10 - 3" x 42" strips, subcut into:

120 - 3" squares (G)

35 - 1 ¾" x 42" strips, subcut into:

120 - 1 ¾" x 4 ¼" rectangles (H)

120 - 1 ¾" x 3" rectangles (I)

240 - 1 ¾" squares (J)

19 - 2 ½" x 42" strips, sew strips end to end and subcut into:

6 - 2 ½" x 90 ½" strips (K)

2 - 2 ½" x 87 ½" strips (L)

Binding 11 - 2 ¼" x 42" strips (M)

The 12th Grade Quilt features the Varsity collection by Sweetwater for Moda Fabrics.

Piecing Instructions:

12th Grade Blocks:

Assemble two Fabric G squares and one Fabric F square.

Rectangle Unit should measure 3" x 8".

Make sixty.

Make sixty.

Assemble two Rectangle Units and one Fabric E rectangle.

Plus Unit should measure 8" x 8".

Make thirty.

Make thirty.

Draw a diagonal line on the wrong side of the Fabric J squares.

With right sides facing, layer a Fabric J square on the bottom right corner of a Fabric A square.

Stitch on the drawn line and trim ¼" away from the seam.

Left Point Unit should measure 4 ¼" x 4 ¼".

Make one hundred twenty.

Make one hundred twenty.

With right sides facing, layer a Fabric J square on the bottom left corner of a Fabric B square.

Stitch on the drawn line and trim ¼" away from the seam.

Right Point Unit should measure 4 ¼" x 4 ¼".

Make one hundred twenty.

Make one hundred twenty.

Draw a diagonal line on the wrong side of the Fabric D squares.

With right sides facing, layer a Fabric D square on the right end of a Fabric H rectangle.

Stitch on the drawn line and trim ¼" away from the seam.

Top Corner Unit should measure 1 ¾" x 4 ¼".

Make one hundred twenty.

Make one hundred twenty.

With right sides facing, layer a Fabric D square on the bottom end of a Fabric I rectangle.

Stitch on the drawn line and trim ¼" away from the seam.

Left Corner Unit should measure 1 ¾" x 3".

Make one hundred twenty.

Make one hundred twenty.

Assemble one Left Corner Unit, one matching Fabric C square and one matching Top Corner Unit.

Corner Unit should measure 4 ¼" x 4 ¼".

Make one hundred twenty.

Make one hundred twenty.

Assemble four matching Corner Units, four matching Left Point Units, four matching Right Point Units and one Plus Unit.

12th Grade Block should measure 15 ½" x 15 ½".

Make thirty.

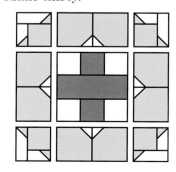 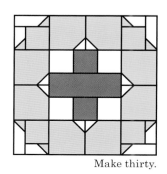

Make thirty.

Quilt Center:

Assemble the Quilt Center.

Quilt Center should measure 83 ½" x 90 ½".

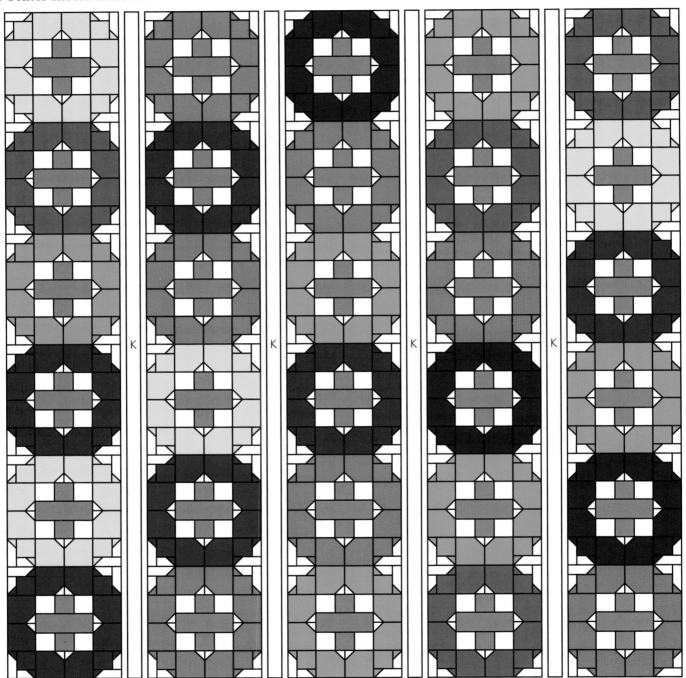

Borders:

Attach side borders using the remaining Fabric K strips.

Attach top and bottom borders using the Fabric L strips.

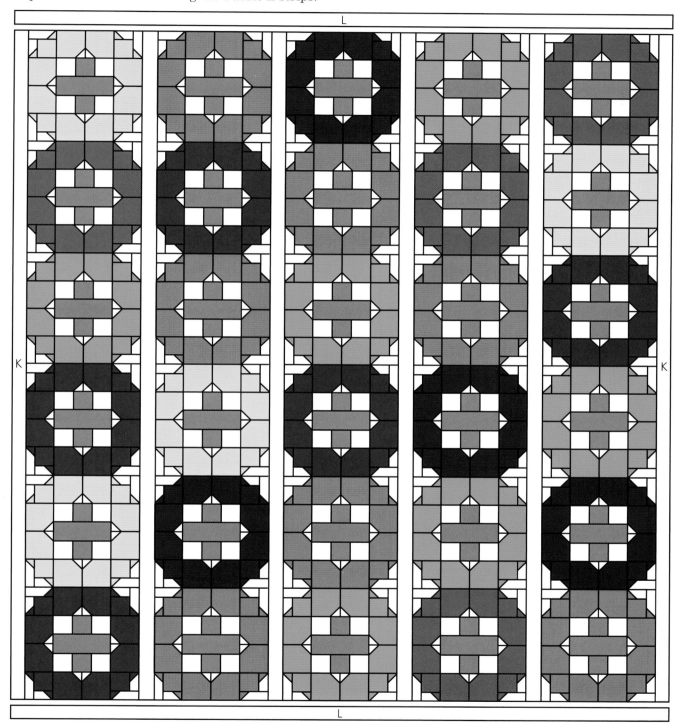

Finishing:

Piece the Fabric M strips end to end for binding.

Quilt and bind as desired.

2nd Grade Quilt

1st Grade Quilt

4th Grade Quilt

3rd Grade Quilt

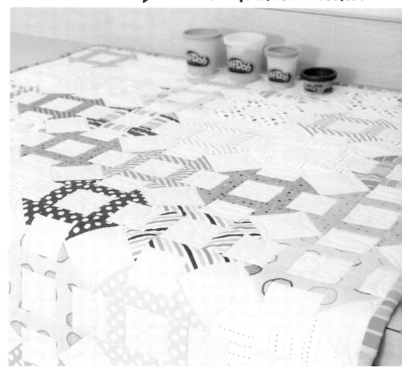

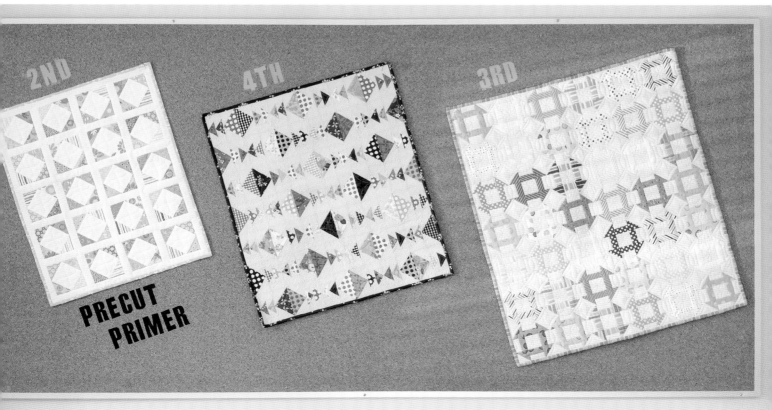

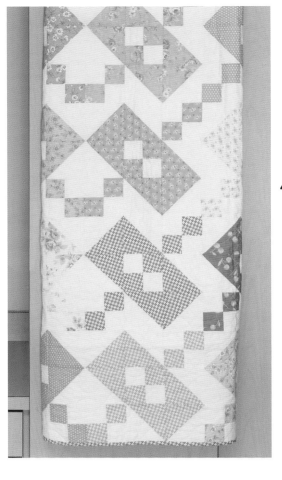

9th Grade Quilt

8th Grade Quilt

5th Grade Quilt